Questions for Ada

Ijeoma Umebinyuo

Drawing in cover photo by Ijeoma Umebinyuo
Cover design by Dragana Nikolic

ISBN-13:978-1505984347
ISBN-10:1505984343

For Chinelo.

Contents

The Genesis

In the beginning
there were women.

remember all the women who wrote for you. all the
women like you, with skin like yours. women who were
once enslaved. women who were once colonized.
women who hold languages that when you try to speak
it, it tears your tongue wide open. remember all these
women who were singers, poets, priestesses, artists,
healers, whose lives were declared anonymous, whose
paintings hang in foreign museums as "unknown"
whose lives declared as unlived. remember them.

do not forget your lineage, do not shrink. do not bend
yourself, do not shift your tongue for anyone.
whenever you forget who you are, remember the
history you have inherited. now, speak.

Confessions

Mother,
I have pasts inside me
I did not bury properly.

Some nights,
your daughter tears herself apart
yet heals in the morning.

For black girls who have to pretend to be strong yet go home breaking down in the middle of the night, trying to breathe. Trying to breathe.

For black girls battling depression. For those who feel so alone in a world telling them this is for whites alone. Please, live.

For black girls who are imperfect, insecure and trying to fit into a world that stifles their voice.

For black girls still learning to glow.

For black girls trying to fit into a world so afraid of their beauty they sell them creams to lighten their skin. For their black skin.

For black girls who smile when they see themselves represented.

Live.
Live.
Live.
Live.

where does depression take you?
Into the night.

what triggers it?
memories.

how do you come out of it?
love.

whose love?
mine.

the delicate acts of survival

you must bring your daughter to church
the devil used her to tempt her uncle
it is the devil that has possessed her
fourteen-year-old body.

when she tells you she hurts,
scold her for tempting men,
make her feel ashamed of her body.

you must bring her to church
for deliverance.

when she is seventeen
and the boys enter her room
she does not go to you

the next day,
your daughter bathes with her pain
her tears a eulogy for their crimes.

the day she sat on the couch
somewhere in London
screaming at the therapist
begging for help
she never mentions it to you.

Ijeoma Umebinyuo

when she is twenty-three
standing
with a degree in her hand
and an unsmiling face
between you and uncle,
she flinches when he moves closer

your daughters sit
sharing memories
one after the other,
revealing a timeline
of secrets.

they are not silent
like their mothers
and they hold their hearts,
curing their pain with love.

your daughter is twenty-five
she called me
begging me to make the depression
go away. go away. go away.
go away. go away. go away.

when your daughter turned thirty
you begged her to make you
a proud mother.

she married him.

broken heart, broken ribs
two miscarriages later

the days she says "no"
he yells ownership of her body
and she lets him.
and she lets him.
and she lets him?

but, remember
your daughter was fourteen
and you begged her
and you begged her
to learn the language of silence.

how quiet can we make this woman?

-   **misogyny**

Tell me,
at night,
do you ever weep for all the women
through stages of your life
you refused to let bloom
all you folded in half,
buried in silence.

Ijeoma Umebinyuo

sister,
there are deaths
stuck between the teeth of my poems.

Nneka

Nne'm, you must forgive me
for all the times I wanted
to love but instead
saw inside
the eyes of men
the ones who held you down
and tore you apart.

A God as woman as me
My sins as painful as hers.

Brave

Even strong women
who fall in love with men
break apart
on the bathroom floor
at a quarter to three a.m.
hugging their knees
and cursing their reflection

Phoenix

One day,
your bones will get weary
of men
who refuse to worship the God in you

On that day,
you will either slit your soul
or gather your spirit,
leaving any man
who has never called you
Holy.

Remember
how your mother kept her bones warm
on nights when your father was far away.

So,
do not love a man who keeps you clinging
to the pillow for too many nights.

Stay away
from men who peel the skin
of other women, forcing you to wear them.

Remember how your mother struggled
to find her skin in the pile.

Do not
scratch your words,
soften your pain, or scrub yourself in shame.

Do not
drown yourself in a man.
He will leave you struggling to breathe.

Survival

I have always wondered
how women who carry war
inside their bones
still grow flowers
between their teeth.

Conversations with Broken Girls

she calls you on the telephone
screaming for help
begging you to come visit her
you sit
she tells you how she loved him
you listen
as she carries herself to memories
she has a faraway look
her skin begins to glow

she says
"men take and take"
you nod in agreement
you hold her hand
as she searches your eyes
for an answer you cannot give
she is smiling as you bring her soup

she has on her lazy smile
and her half-moon gaze
men have always
loved her
for her sugar smile,
consuming her high

you ask her if it hurts
she does not reply
she says
"he loved how my skin felt against his"
she has a faraway look,

gathering her pain
for another lonely night

you ask her again
she does not reply
she says with pain stretching her voice
"i already had baby names"
and you hear the walls wail.

twice broken,
three times more powerful.

The woman
carried herself
like God
worshipped her body.

Even the devil
will pray for forgiveness
at the holy sight of her.

Nobody warned you
that the women whose feet
you cut from running
would give birth to
daughters with wings.

Ijeoma Umebinyuo

I needed myself and I found her.

Your son does not know
how to love a woman
without
trying to erase her from herself,
without
trying to burn her into ashes,
without
trying to possess her body.

Nne

I am stitching her heart back
please, visit another day

I am taking away the tears slowly
emptying her sorrow
please, visit another day

I am walking her into sunshine
gathering her beauty
please, visit another day

I am stitching her heart back
She is steadily holding my hands
She no longer weeps.

She is beginning to find her smile
on the face of her daughter.

Cruel

forcing manhood
on boys with skin
still soft and sticking
to mother's milk for survival
is cruel.

Bless the daughters who sat,
carrying the trauma of mothers.

Who sat asking for more love
and not getting any,
carried themselves into the morning

Bless the daughters who were given the role of
motherhood before they became women.
Bless the daughters who raised themselves.

Your mother was your first mirror.

Tell me,

didn't she carry herself well enough
to make you feel like a God?

Ijeoma Umebinyuo

There are many ways to love yourself
without breaking in half for a man.
Even your mother forgot to teach herself.

Where have you been all your life?

Ijeoma Umebinyuo

The Wives

When your husband returns
reeking of his lover's perfume
do not question him.

When his lies fill the room,
soaking up the air,
his easy smile painting his face,
you gather yourself with a smile.

You prepare his favorite meal,
you oil your skin,
you lower the light from the oil lamp,
you let him enter you
as you watch his shadow shake,
but
remember not to scream
his brother's name.

You are twenty-two,
the boy you let love you
has had enough of your sugar
so, you label yourself
"unwanted"
as you begin to feel
in the dark,
pinching your body,
apologizing
for all your extras.

Ijeoma Umebinyuo

Bottled Memories

She is a collection of sighs and worries,
her being pieced together
with too many unspoken goodbyes

Poem No. 1

I did not know
the bodies of women
were meant to be
a museum of tragedies,
as if we were meant to carry the ocean
without drowning

wounds filled with love.
woman becoming.

for imperfect daughters
for those who do not
bow to tradition

for imperfect daughters
still trying each day
not to call themselves failures

you are here. you are becoming.
isn't that enough?

Ijeoma Umebinyuo

Survive

Some women survive
by growing claws on their skin,
pinching whomever comes,
examining them
before cutting their claws off
to be liquid love.

Don't curse them
for when the attacker came;
she was liquid first
and has just learnt her lesson.

Some women survive
by creating walls,
big walls guarding their hearts
and you say,
"let them in"
but
she has been covered in regrets,
crawled on all fours for her salvation.

Don't curse them
for when her attacker came
there she was, loving, now
she has built her walls
brick by brick
guarding against parasites.

Don't blame her.

Some women are broken
not ready to be healed,
some women are broken
not ready for love,
and that's all right.

Let her find herself.
Let her crawl if she must.
Let her tear herself apart.
Let her question all she knows.
Let her become her own sun.
Let her.

Ijeoma Umebinyuo

Miscarriage

Chinazor lost her baby two months ago.
Her husband hates
when she accuses him of
finding pleasures in another woman
So he raised his fist,
and she woke up in the hospital
with him kneeling,
pleading for her forgiveness.

She moved into her father's house
as neighbors ask her mother
when she will go back to her husband
And her mother tells them,
"Tomorrow…tomorrow…"
with a smile like an apology
for having a daughter
whose being does not include
shifting her value
for a man.

Chinazor lost her baby two months ago.
Her husband hates
when she accuses him of
finding pleasures in another woman
So he raised his fist,
and she woke up in the hospital
with him kneeling,
pleading for her forgiveness.

Poem No. 2

The woman, alone,
finding parts of herself
she never knew existed
will always be more powerful.

Memories

The old man
carries the memories
of his wife in his smile

He dreams of her
in the white wedding dress
stained with the kind of soil
only found in Botswana

His face wrinkled
hiding histories
showing lives lived
his hands hard from planting.

The farmer who used to
carry crops to the city.

The old man
carries the memories
of his wife in his smile
he dreams of her
in the white wedding dress
sewn by her mother
worn by her
stained with the kind of soil
found only in Botswana.

Chewing Flowers

I am writing for the women
who were once girls
judging themselves
through the eyes
of souls
who couldn't comprehend
their light

I am writing for the women
who stammered
just to speak
and
who forced themselves
into silence
when ugly words
were once thrown at them

I am writing for the women
who keep kneeling
screaming at their phone
as lovers leave
as friends depart

I am writing for
all these women
who still show up
with a smile
after battling their demons
the night before

Ijeoma Umebinyuo

I am also writing
for the women
who do not smile
the next day

Women who
need
a day or two
to recover
from the brutalities
of the world

Poem No. 3

We are writing
for our mothers' mothers
and
their mothers
we are writing
for our daughters
and
the daughters of our daughters
we are writing
for our ancestors
and
generations to come

Just like that,
you began to love
all the women in you
they shamed.

Just like that,
you slowly began to love
the little girl in you
they scarred.

Just like that,
you began to love
the girl who opened her legs
and made love to the first man
who did not sneak in at night.
Although the next morning
he called you a whore,
you began to love her.

You began to love
all the women
inside you
and you began to nurse her
back into life
without apologizing
for how she heals herself.

Freedom

Your feminism
wears a wrapper,
cooks for her husband,
changed her surname.

Ijeoma Umebinyuo

You are beautiful
like yourself

Love Letter to Adeyemi

Dear Yemi, remember how to weep without filling your blood with pain. You must remember never to cut your hair out of anger. You must remember never to curse at the person staring at you through the mirror, even when you cannot remember her face, even when her eyes hold an ocean of pain. You must remember how to hold yourself back from hurting others when your anger swells into days. You must learn how to heal yourself when the nights make it seem impossible.

You must remember how to sing yourself away from sorrows, how to wash yourself till the sadness weeps out of your body. You must remember to hold yourself on days that feel so empty the pain echoes. You are a woman, a vast land filled with holy cities. You are a woman becoming. You are a song to your mother, a city filled with landmarks of joy.

You are a woman,
a vast land,
a holy city.

Ijeoma Umebinyuo

You teach your daughters
how to rub poison on their skin
remember
to teach your sons
how not to be serpents

Confession

i came to you
as a wildflower
as a woman who has passed
through different stages
of her womanhood
to know not even the
sweetest man
deserves my silence

you are not holy water.

        flawed as i am,
        i am not a sin.

Ijeoma Umebinyuo

I have organized all my fears,
we are having a rally tonight.

Please, come, attend.

write a poem for your fourteen-year-old self.
forgive her. heal her. free her.

Ijeoma Umebinyuo

The way women are told
to carry pain in their bones
frightens me.

The Concubine

Chinelo cooks jollof rice
for her husband just the way
he loves it
with enough ground dry chili pepper.

She hand-washes his underwear
and removes the wrinkles from his clothes with
with the expensive Black & Decker pressing iron
she bought in London.

She has eagerly joined the league of newly married
women in Lekki.

Three months after her master's program in London
was over,
her wedding was featured in
one of those Nigerian wedding blogs
after her friends told her
it was not a wedding till blogs showed her wedding
dress, her wedding smile, and
readers read about her perfect wedding story.

She learnt how to make his body
shake inside her;
she waxed underneath as her sister had advised.

Ijeoma Umebinyuo

She cooked his food with a little less spice
when her husband's preference changed.

She brought a housemaid
so on days when she returns late from work
she can shower and only have to wait
for him to return.

She checked the blogs
then learnt to go down,
raising his manhood
just like her sister told her to do.

He came home two nights ago
on their second wedding anniversary
she made love to him
and patiently waited
for him to shake inside her
however,
nothing prepared Chinelo
for the name he called out
while he slept.

The next morning,
she gathered her clothes quietly,
bought a bus ticket for the housemaid.
Everyone knows a concubine
cannot compete with the wife
under the same roof.

Broken

This is what you tell your best friend still screaming into the night on days when she remembers. You must tell her she is a garden of light. You must listen to her cry and not interrupt her. You plant flowers inside your words, you must listen to her pain. You must not let her die screaming her pains outside her body.

This is what you must tell your friend when she calls you, unable to sleep, wanting for the darkness to go.

She wants to feel normal again. You must sit, place her head on your thigh, then you must sing to her. This is what you do when she calls telling you how she tried living but the pain keeps coming back; you must remember to plant flowers inside the words you give her. You must call her a survivor, you must tell her she is loved, you must never let her go.

You must show her light.

Ijeoma Umebinyuo

Ulo

I will return home to six graves
with a foreign accent
I will kneel and greet each of them
waiting for them to bless me
I will return home to six graves
sitting where I was once
just a little girl
I will imagine her dancing to welcome me
offering me roasted yam and peppered palm oil
I will remember their smiles
she will remember me
even with my foreign accent
she will still speak Igbo
but
I will return home to five graves
to ancestors who held me as a baby
telling me who I was once in my former life
I will return home to five graves
with a foreign accent
where Obianuju means
she came in abundance
I will return home
as half-eaten love poems
never a foreigner,
always the daughter of her people.

this is your springtime,
your joy is blooming
where thorns wilt.

Ijeoma Umebinyuo

I keep finding
my mother
in parts of me
I never knew existed.

Glory

Before the year ends,
teach yourself five things
your mother never taught you
then, teach yourself five things
you want to teach your daughter.

Miracle

You gave a woman the sea, thinking she will drown.
She sieved the sea to make sugar. Magic!

Five Languages

You carry five languages in your tongue.

The first you learnt at eight
when he called you away from your siblings
and taught you why some men
who smile at little girls
make you uncomfortable.
You painfully learnt the secret language of mistrust.

The second language you learnt
at ten years old
when your uncle said,
"You will never be
as beautiful as your light-skinned sister."
You heard your mother cry
five years later,
as you begged her
to make your skin
just a little lighter
for you had learnt the language of self-hate.

The third language you learnt
when you saw your auntie
go back to her husband
the one Umuada chastised
for hitting her.
She told you,
"A woman is nothing without a man,"
her eyes gathering tears
and you learnt

the language of helplessness.

The fourth language you learnt
when he kissed you at twenty
and you flinched.
He asked,
"What are you scared of?"
You didn't tell him
how fluent your tongue is
with the language of mistrust.
"You are a virgin?"
he asked,
and you saw the glee in his eyes.
That moment,
you learnt another language,
the language of power.

The fifth language you learnt
at twenty-five
when your friends
brought you offerings of darkness
and you painfully peeled your skin
to reveal another being
learning
the language of change.

Poem No. 4

You call me
"sister"
not because
you are my blood
but because
you understand
the kind of tragedies
we both have endured
to come back into
loving ourselves
again
and
again.

Pain

Forgive me, father
but sometimes my God
is a woman
sitting on the kitchen floor
her hands holding her legs
screaming for help
without making a sound.

Forgive me, father
but sometimes my God
is a woman
calling me on the phone
begging me to call her
"beautiful"
because her lover forced
ugliness into her soul.

Forgive me, father
but sometimes my God
is a woman
crying in the shower
begging for another God
to lift her burden.

Tell me:
now you are here,
will you wither or bloom?

Ijeoma Umebinyuo

Water the poem
cut it in half,
feed it to yourself.

so many women
so many women
whose blood i carry
so many glorious lives
living inside me.

Ijeoma Umebinyuo

slowly,
learn to outgrow
some souls,
even your old self

Ancestors

Descendants of women
who wore head wraps
changed their surnames
bowed their heads
lowered their eyes
painted their bodies
gave birth
carried our fathers
on their backs with wrapper
farmed with their husbands

On Eke market days
went to the market to sell,
business women

On Nkwo market days
walked a few kilometers
carrying our fathers
fetching water with calabash
calabash made from clay

On Orie, she cooked his
favorite meal
her day, his last wife
he loved her skin
called her Nmachi,
beauty of God

On one Afor market day,
she bore him a daughter
"Ngozi," they called her.

Descendants of mothers
who wore head wraps
lowered their eyes
bowed their heads
changed their surnames
descendants of women
whose husbands
never went to war
without their blessing.

I curated our love into poems
and all the pains became less
all the anger left, eventually
but, there is no denying
there was a loving here
inside my heart,
with scars still healing,
that I once loved a man.

Narratives

Our mothers
our great-grandmothers
all the women whose blood
we carry.

All of them
and none of them
needed to be saved
by someone who
called them exotic
or tries to write their guilt
away by researching them.

All our mothers have
always known the power
of sisterhood;
you didn't teach them
how to use their weapons.

You look like my next love poem.

Ijeoma Umebinyuo

sometimes,
the poems arrive
in the body of a lover.

my love has been known to perform miracles.

Ijeoma Umebinyuo

Your lover
has a sneaky way
of hiding her poems:
inside her mouth
on her neck
between her thighs.

you are not weak
you are just tired
for now.

you are not quitting
i know you
i know you

you are just resting,
darling.

Dew

She taught her lover
to understand the language
of climaxing women.
Now, he comes daily,
seeking to taste spring water.

I guess this is how April feeds May.

Your Women

she said to her lover,
i know outside feels
like every ink
the universe used
to paint your skin
is a mistake
but
these thick thighs
and these full lips
still know you

she said to her lover,
i know they've tried
to break the man
away from you,
calling you
everything
but human

i am your whole
i stood with you
through centuries
i will not leave you now

bring your bloody knuckles
i will wash them
yet heat the furnace
for us to fight again

i will guard you
on days when you know
your manhood needs
to feel its softness

she said,
these legs
will carry you home
will feed you
and
i will sing you songs of
freedom

I am too full of life
to be half-loved.

Ijeoma Umebinyuo

Bad Habits

His name on my tongue
tastes like mango
the kind we used to pick
as we sneaked into
our neighbor's house
giggling with joy
at the sight of its ripeness

will you survive?

no, darling, I will thrive.

Poem No. 5

Healing comes in waves
and maybe today
the wave hits the rocks
and that's okay,
that's okay, darling
you are still healing
you are still healing.

It is still winter
carry yourself gently
you are honey
you are flowers
you are enough.

October

You married the man
who still has my name
clinging to his tongue
so,
I am sorry for nights
he carries me to the bed
yet is inside you

You should know
how to quietly cry
after lovers who leave.

You should learn
how to move your feet
till it dances
and you must learn to fly
away from the pain.

You must learn how
to do all these things
and live through the day
without hurting yourself.

Remember, the day he marries another
the day he calls
begging for you to forgive him,
you must remember to move your feet
you must remember to dance
and you must remember how to fly.

coconut oil
&
whipped shea butter
&
peppermint oil
&
my lover's touch
&
our bodies
&
our glorious blackness

I am learning to be patient
with my healing
and never to close my mouth
when my scars scream.

I am learning to be patient
with my healing
and never to carry fire
when all I want to do is
feast on water and silence.

Ijeoma Umebinyuo

You did not carry yourself
away from pain
to become pain itself.

A little kinder, darling.
A little softer, sweetheart.

Do you return from love
as yourself or as another?
It seems there are still women
I have to become
to understand the woman I was.

Ijeoma Umebinyuo

Stay,
you are beginning to glow

I still have
some poems to feed you.

Where the sun rises

mother blushes
when she speaks of father
she rolls her eyes
giggles and says his name
with so much softness
taking time to taste it
i watch her begin to laugh
when he describes
the young shy woman she was
she looks at him with so much longing
"Nkem"
she says, as father holds her hand
"my own"
she translates to English
"Nneoma"
father replies
"beautiful mother"
i say softly

Ijeoma Umebinyuo

The problem was
you kept checking for flaws
in places where he felt
needed less of you
like, your face
like, your body
like, your voice.
The problem was
you kept waiting for another
to call you powerful.

You naively believed men like him
were capable of loving
women who make
crowns from thorns.

The problem was
you loved him so shamelessly,
even his lies became holy.

Questions for Ada

Ada, are you in love?
Yes.
Is being in a relationship hard work?
Yes.
Do you write love poems for your lover?
Every day.
Does your lover believe in you?
Yes, but sometimes I fear my lover does not
comprehend her light.
What do you do on those days?
I bathe her, I play her some jazz,
I feed her, I weep for her.
Describe her in a sentence.
Her eyes carry strength,
her words scratch, she speaks love.
Ada, are you in love?
Yes.
Is being in a relationship hard work?
Yes.
Who is your lover?
Myself.

Tunde

You
leave you on my skin
my friends know you visited
they keep mapping your visit
on my skin

They say
he was there last night,
on her neck,
around her thighs,
even her words
soak with pleasure

Desert

He made love to you
while trying to find her,
looked at you
as though your eyes would
reveal the reason
for her departure.
Kissed you like your lips
were burning with her name;
your moans gathering,
he tried to find her tune.
You stayed, didn't you?
Tried to show him
what lies within you
is better than what she offered.
You held his head
and looked into his eyes,
screaming in anger
"I am here! I am here! Look at me!"
And darling,
you soon learnt
she branded her being
through his blood
to the beginning of his soul.
You foolishly
offered flowers
to a man
seeking water.

Ijeoma Umebinyuo

Stay
let me tell you
how salt fell in love

one day,
salt found water
and just would not let go.

- Ocean

Ijeoma Umebinyuo

are you shrinking yourself again, darling?

you have always known
how to win yourself back
from wars

you come to me
a broken verse
and like a
repetition of old sins
I offer you
the high rise of my body

Blood

You found parts of your ancestors inside you,
In your dance, in your poems, in your language
You found parts, bits and pieces of your ancestors
Even those that drowned in the ocean.

Ijeoma Umebinyuo

Daughters do not have to inherit
the silence of their mothers.

there are love poems
on the edges of my skin
i watch my lover
gently kiss them into freedom

Ijeoma Umebinyuo

Naked before my eyes,
I thank whatever gods created your ancestors.

He said,
"You are beautiful."
I told him
"beautiful"
is a lazy and lousy way to describe me.

some people
are what you try
to write away

trying to forget
the lingering taste of betrayal
that still burns your throat

at three a.m.
they are what the fabrics of your insomnia
weave wickedly for you

colonization now wrapped
in different gifts.
we killed our brothers
over country lines.
there lies a river of pain,
look at our bloody hands
we have tried to come up
with another song for our land
but there are jails
for those who do not
sing the songs of the oppressors.

Ijeoma Umebinyuo

Omowale

Amidst all your yesterdays
you stand up, stronger.
When there was no light
your soul lit your spirit.

In the pains of uncertainty
you seek life.

Therein lies it all.

I will scream your name,
I will dance.

Everyone will know
you have come to feel the warm hugs
of your sister

You smile like I remember when you were seven
The cashew tree we used to climb is still there

If you cry,
we would cry.

But please, Omowale
do not feast us only sweet tales
for we felt your scars when we hugged you.

you do not mourn the living
not the man who once promised you
his love
you do not mourn the living
not the friend who left you
when you were so helpless
do not mourn the lover
do not mourn anyone
not a living human
who did not see
the love you poured
do not make yourself
a graveyard.

Ijeoma Umebinyuo

The Returnee

You wear your
short skirts
while speaking
with an accent
so foreign to your people.

You carry your camera
with eyes of pity
telling everyone
how much freedom
they are missing.

You roll your eyes
when the waiter forgets
to add the extra slice of lemon
in your water.

You seek big vocabularies
to explain
how nothing just works
in the land of your father.

You sit in traffic
in your air-conditioned car
cursing the horrible traffic

You tell your driver
he needs to speak proper English
and not his pidgin English
with a Yoruba accent

You are on the phone
with your friend from London
she laughs at the silliness of it all,
at the "backwardness" of your
homeland

You do not notice
how no one has ever asked
for you to spell your name

See how
shamelessly you have forgotten
whose breasts nourished you.

Ijeoma Umebinyuo

For the foreign-educated returnee

The day your education makes you roll your eyes at
your father, the day your exposure makes you call your
own mother uncivilized, the day your amazing foreign
degrees make you cringe as your driver speaks pidgin
English, may you never forget your grandfather was a
farmer from Oyo State who never understood English.

aching hearts//missing home

At the embassy,
they never warned us about days
America will feel so lonely
we will gather our mother tongue,
hastily swallowing words
that remind us of home to keep warm

Ijeoma Umebinyuo

Like you,
I am tired of waking up to news of death.

Cousin,
 in this country you cannot hide your blackness
anywhere
you cannot remove it. you cannot cover it.
sometimes a burden and bull's-eye.

Ijeoma Umebinyuo

Cry

America, while you were asleep
another woman mourned her
dead black lover's
bullet-ridden body,
as his baby cried for
her father's life.

the happiness when it comes,
when it stays,
my goodness it makes you look so beautiful

come closer.

you are living
you are breathing
perhaps a bit hurt
perhaps a bit pained
but
you are breathing
you are breathing
and that is enough to wake
the angels still living
in your chest.

Prodigal

When they call you, telling you how they wish you were
never born. You listen to them call you a failure. You
quietly cut the call and strip naked. You walk into your
bathroom and turn on the shower. You cry your heart
out. You come out dripping of swallowed excuses. You
call me as you kneel on the bathroom floor, telling me
how badly you want to live. I tell you to hold on, I tell
you sometimes the moon is too weak to be full. Today,
there are just too many clouds. Just today. You say how
weak your life has gotten. I listen to you curse God. I
do not correct you. These suns don't come easy
anymore. I watch you peel your skin in silence. I watch
you fight your fight in anger. You say "yellow," and I
say joy. You say "God," baby, I say you.

Ijeoma Umebinyuo

Boys Quarter

My neighbor said
to the woman
the one who traveled
from Lagos
to Onitsha

She said
"My daughter will be good,
very good, she can cook
and she can wash"
The woman looks at my neighbor
with a pasted smile
the kind of smile
rich people give to poor people
a bit condescending
a bit patronizing

Little girl gets into the big red car
the woman is a rich madam
she brings bags of rice from
the boot of the car
she promises that little girl will visit

My neighbor called her daughter aside
in whispered voice, tells her to be a big girl
to remember she is from a good name
to never forget to do as she is told
to remember she will be an example
to her brothers and sisters

Little girl waves at me
I hug her
she is only thirteen
with skinny fingers
that love to play
yet stern to her younger siblings.

But little girl was broken
the madam from Lagos
would add pepper to water,
making a paste,
putting it into her eyes

When she forgets
how to add enough salt to the food
madam from Lagos
would run around the house
with a cane
calling her a witch
her clothes torn from lashes

So, little girl remembered
she is a big girl
and from a good home
an example to her siblings
she held the dark events in
"Tomorrow, I go do am well ma"
she promised her madam
as she knelt, begging for her sympathy

Ijeoma Umebinyuo

That night
little girl slept with a machete
when the madam walked in
she screamed at the sight
of her husband
with his trousers down to his knees
half naked,
dead
beside
little girl.

I beat my heart
till it became unconscious
last night.

This morning
my mother
showed me our scars,
multiple wounds
on her body.

Forgive your mother
for all the miracles she couldn't perform.

I am
stretching
my hands
towards my mother
she is clinging to me
like salt to water
we will heal this wound
and to the terrifying distance
we will bridge
like birthing me again
this time, I watch her
and help her cut the umbilical cord.

Ijeoma Umebinyuo

The Wash

Kwame has beautiful dark skin
his teeth gloriously white
in primary five
he returned home one day
begging not to go back to school
his accent thick like smog in Accra

Ghana on his tongue
he loved to laugh
and he loved to dance
slowly, Kwame stopped
speaking out loud
when the little kids laughed
at the way he pronounced "water"

Kwame stopped
dancing when animal noises
were made by his classmates
but
Kwame has beautiful dark skin
his teeth gloriously white
his mother begged him to tell her
why he calls her food disgusting

Kwame
changed his name to "Steve"
in school
but still he couldn't fit in

He scrubbed his skin
till it was sore
still he glowed like his ancestors

One day, his mother
saw Kwame
kneeling beside his bed
begging God
to make his midnight skin color go away.

Nkem

he comes to me,
a broken man
and i tell him to sit still
so i can pick the sadness away
from his soft skin.

when he is near
when he touches me
when my name spills
out of his lips

when he is a sinner
when he is holy
when he is broken
when he is soft
this his love—like music

i have witnessed in my mother
i witnessed in my father
how to love between cities
and cry when weak

i witnessed in my mother
i witnessed in my father
how to carry yourself home
no matter how far away we go

The Clinic

You are twenty years old
standing by the stop
smelling of fast food
soul full of immigrant dreams
your class at two p.m.
you missed more hours
for MoneyGram
for your little sister
needs to take her exam
to enter the University of Lagos

you are twenty-three years old
sitting beside him
he stands up,
you watch him walk naked
his skin contrast against yours
he reminds you of
rain in August back in Lagos
the kind of rain that floods
the roads, that blocks the
entrance to your street

four days ago
you listened as your father said
"everyone is so proud of you
you are such a great daughter
keep working and focusing on school"

you try not to let the darkness break you down
as you hold yourself from falling

Ijeoma Umebinyuo

sometimes
home seems so far away
you will desperately cradle
anyone
even if they flood your spirit
like the rains in Lagos

you walk quietly into the clinic
your rosary in your pocket
praying to Mary
trying your hardest not to
touch your belly
as the doctor calls your name

be brave
or this storm
will sink your
beautiful heart

Ijeoma Umebinyuo

do not believe
those who will
dull the brightness of the moon
from their neighbor's sky
yet sit outside their homes
counting the stars

Crawl back into yourself,
warm your bones.

Write yourself a love poem,
welcome yourself home.

Be kind to your body,
for it has won so many wars.

Ijeoma Umebinyuo

broken apart so many times
God uses me for lectures

Teach yourself
never to join the parade
of souls
who think picking themselves apart
will make them a bit more lovable.

Teach yourself
to leave
wherever you are tolerated.

Ijeoma Umebinyuo

use their hate
as an ointment
to glow even more

let them wonder
how people like you
they have tried
to break
still shine

water for fire
honey for wounds
flowers for my soul
kindness for your hate
burnt my anger into joy

Ijeoma Umebinyuo

you are not alive
to please the aesthetic
of colonized eye.

are you shrinking yourself again, darling?

Ijeoma Umebinyuo

Be

Where
your soul
cracks open
to reveal flaws,
plant flowers.

Questions for Ada

We are aware
of the many reasons
to fall apart
to break apart
to never rise again
but we have lived in the glory
of standing with our face
towards the sun again and again.

Self

Your body
has scars
of regrets
mix
some salt
and water
here
bless you
back into life

Beneath it all
I know
you are made of soft wind
and calm flowing water
but
on days when
you become strong wind
and crashing waves
be rest assured
you did not
become less of you

do not become the woman
apologizing for days
when she has thorns
from the harshness
of the world.

Someone should have told you
the eyes of a lover are not where
you find your beauty.

Someone should have told you
never to cling to another
for a reason to feel precious.

he held your body
pouring his words

staining you

it has taken you years
to wash yourself clean,
to adore yourself again.

Ijeoma Umebinyuo

she is
carrying herself
into her baptism
renaming herself
finding her tongue

she is woven out of soft skin,
she is clinging to water.

Sugar skin,
protect yourself from souls
who only come to feast
on your light,
leaving you with darkness.

Ijeoma Umebinyuo

Jos

The harmattan season had already begun,
Saturday just waking up.
Ogechi ate moin moin
and akamu with her auntie.

She calls me from the kiosk of
the woman who sells recharge cards.
The woman's first son
has taken a liking to Ogechi;
she tells me how much she loves
this part of the North
and she laughs
when the boy walks in.

She tells me boys love when you laugh.
So, there was Ogechi laughing
like a little rooster
but
softening her voice
in his presence;
boys love that too,
she tells me.
"I am enjoying my holiday,
my dear, Jos is so beautiful,"
she says as she hangs up.

Questions for Ada

That day,
she visits her auntie's store
and dances around
to some Aaliyah,
her favorite artist,
that day,
she laughs a little louder
when her auntie teases her
about her breasts getting bigger.

The fight began somewhere
a few stores away.
The youths decided to take
matters into their own hands,
asking how you pray
to know if today
will be your last.

The next day,
I knelt before God
cursing everyone
who stood by
and watched
as Ogechi
cried for her mother.

Ada, are you afraid?
I was.
Why were you afraid?
They do not look like me.
Why are you no longer afraid?
The girls like me will see me.

-    **representation**

Obioma

You carry ancient languages in your tongue.
Six nights ago, you tried cutting your ties to darkness,
your international phone cards ripped on the floor,
as you screamed the names of God
in four different languages.

Your mother called.
You imagine her feet stained with Enugu red soil,
what you would do for a Sunday of harmattan,
chapped lips, and sweet rice.

Your father came back
a soldier from peacekeeping
with a callused heart
left somewhere between Sierra Leone and Liberia;
he says war grinds pain into souls.

One night,
you saw him speaking to himself
screaming his anger ,
eating the moon for dinner.

Two days ago,
you were called to rush back home
Your mother was found with her wrapper around her
neck, the red and yellow one
she wore to the airport
waving as you left for America.

You heard your father say,
"Some demons cannot be fought in one lifetime."
All you remembered was how
pained she looked.

Ajayi

Quiet like nighttime in Ondo,
vibrant like the night market in Ibadan,
men would prostrate before her
bringing gifts to appease her.

Ifa priestesses predicted
children would dance in her womb
they forgot to tell her
her son will turn mad after
eighteen full moons,
they forgot to tell her
her daughter will fly away again and again
past midnight.

Two full moons after her daughter's last birth
she waited patiently,
applying towel dipped and squeezed in cold water
on her baby's warm feverish body,
then the bird came
calling for her daughter.

Ajayi threw the white powder as instructed,
muttering words, calling on all her ancestors as
instructed by the priestess.

The bird fell;
cutlass held tight,
blood splattered on her face,
she washed herself with the water from the calabash
and buried the bird underneath the ash
from last night's firewood.

The next morning,
the town crier announced
the river moved to the next village.

Maternity

After her husband broke the window with his fist, your
mother begged your auntie to sew herself new skin.
She slowly swallows her garri, her eyes staring at the
walls. There was only the kerosene lamp flickering; you
trace their shadows with your finger as you listen to
your mother ask her why. She takes her time to
swallow, she tries to speak and you watch her shadow
begin to shake. Your mother's shadow slowly moves.
You watched in wonder as the shadows become one.
You hear the hurt in your auntie's voice. She has just
arrived from Benin with her unborn baby almost dying.
She will go back on Monday; she will give birth to
Chioma, leaving her with her life.

Ijeoma Umebinyuo

Alone

Your auntie begged God for a husband
her morning ritual
included a quiet prayer for a man
to come change her last name.

One evening
as she placed a sanitary pad on her panties
she told you she might start to bleach her skin,
slyly rolling the words off her tongue.

Three years later
you catch her laughter
as she speaks
so excited to stop being a spinster
she begs you to come visit.

You visit.
You notice the forced smile
in the wedding photographs
you notice how the walls got so cold
as he does not find warmth between her thighs.
It was her second miscarriage.

You visit.
You heard her begging for another chance
you overheard her telling her friends
"Some nights, he returns
with the smell of that woman—that jezebel."

They said,
"Stay, endure.
He is your husband,
you endure."

And the last thing you remembered
was how even in death
she seemed to be carrying herself
alone
to her
creator.

Ijeoma Umebinyuo

they look at you
like you should
apologize
for how your body
holds sadness
inside your eyes.

so many broken children
living in grown bodies,
mimicking adult lives.

Ijeoma Umebinyuo

Leave your words
to marinate on paper.
Come back and taste it,
how does it taste?

Land

Out of darkness
angels are born;
remember that when
your demons call you
to play.

The tired marks on your skin
are beginning to show,
your pasted smiles
are frightening your reflection.

Lover, refuse the urge to tear you apart
The vultures hovering around
will die of starvation
I promise.

.

Ijeoma Umebinyuo

Before creating you
The Universe washed her hands.
"This will take time,"
she said
as she closed her days.

Your cousin came home from the war
like a broken flower
wanting to be exhumed and brought back to life.

He tells you about the dead he saw
their mouth open with abandoned stories
still living in their chests, begging to be free.

Ijeoma Umebinyuo

there are ways to let the world kill you.
first, lose your tongue in the mouth of a lover.
second, do not remember your softness.

come as you are
cracked hearts
rebellious soul
soft words
mistakes
scarred being
full belly laughter
sing to me in the language of your soul
unmask your fears
beside mine, lay yours there
come as you are
do not plaster your walls
with nothing but truths

Ijeoma Umebinyuo

Lover,
place your hands
on my skin,
find heat.

This is how
you warm your soul
in winter.

Secrets

Your mother is still praying
for the day you will stop
rejecting the marriage proposals.

She holds her breasts
as she asks why
you cannot see
a child has to be
fed through yours
just as she fed you.

"Every woman needs a man,"
she says softly,
her voice trying not to break
begging you to reconsider
begging to save her face
for what will she tell people?

You are an Igbo woman.
Her first daughter. Her Ada.

She wants you to carry
the joys in your womb
just like she carried you
but
you still haven't told her
about your best friend
the one she calls your sister
you still haven't told her
she keeps your bed warm

Ijeoma Umebinyuo

I don't think you understand
some chose life last night
even if they never tell you,
they just killed
their demons
to live this morning.

where does politics end
and your love poems begin?
sometimes, they are both the same thing
sometimes, they have to be the same thing.

Ijeoma Umebinyuo

Diaspora blues

So,
here you are
too foreign for home
too foreign for here.
Never enough for both.

First Generation

Here's to the security guards who maybe had a degree in another land. Here's to the manicurist who had to leave her family to come here, painting the nails, scrubbing the feet of strangers. Here's to the janitors who don't even understand English yet work hard despite it all. Here's to the fast-food workers who work hard to see their family smile. Here's to the laundry man at the Marriott who told me with the sparkle in his eyes how he was an engineer in Peru.

Here's to the bus driver, the Turkish Sufi who almost danced when I quoted Rumi. Here's to the harvesters who live in fear of being deported for coming here to open the road for their future generation. Here's to the taxi drivers from Nigeria, Ghana, Egypt, and India who gossip amongst themselves.

Here's to them waking up at 4 a.m., calling home to hear the voices of their loved ones. Here's to their children, to the children who despite it all become artists, writers, teachers, doctors, lawyers, activists, and rebels. Here's to international money transfers. For never forgetting home.

Here's to their children who carry the heartbeats of their motherland and even in sleep, speak with pride about their fathers. Keep on.

Ijeoma Umebinyuo

i wanted to write a love poem

i wanted to write
a love poem
but i was carrying
too many news of deaths
inside my blood.

i wanted to write
a love poem
but i came home
too tired and too pained
to remove all the sighs
covering my bed.

Anger

sit still.

let me remove
the thunder brewing
inside your veins

Ulomma, on the first page of your journal, you must write, "This body has carried herself into days so bitter all gods wept. Yet, I am still here and I will always be here." Then, you begin to write about it.

On the third day of the sixth month, when your heart is too tired to feel alive, reference the first page of your journal.

On the eighth month, when your friend hurts you and all you have left are words that scratch your hands, bleed as you write. But write this: "I know that it seems impossible, even my hands move when I bleed. I am healing." Then, pour every single pain into your journal and write. Write till your heart feels alive again.

On the eleventh month, when the sun swells up and drops a little bit of sunshine, write about the sun like you just met it, like you just discovered how it left your body to find room in the sky.

(i)
the sharp twisted tongue of your mother
the unpleasant presence of your father
the words thrown across the room
deafening

(ii)
the stink of ugly surrounding you

(iii)
the neighbors came
pulling your mother
from the hands of your father

(iv)
carry yourself to the ocean
carry yourself to the ocean
the ground has become too hard
drown your yesterdays,
baptize their sins.

You are made
of
water
distance
dreams
mother's tears
father's pain
broken tongue
forced language
colonized eyes
bastardized religions

Ijeoma Umebinyuo

You lost cultures
You lost language
You lost religions
You lost it all in the fire
that is colonization
So, do not apologize
for owning every piece of you
they could not take,
break,
and claim as theirs.

Irony

they invite you
to come view
artifacts
stolen
from
your
ancestors
in their museums
as their
"experts"
explain
your
ancient
Benin
kingdom

Ijeoma Umebinyuo

The Baptism

Excuse me,
but you cannot have
"Obianuju"
as her baptismal name,
but here
are a number of
European saints
you can choose from—
how about Agnes?

No, I do not know
what it means,
but "Obianuju"
cannot be used.

God will not understand it.

Yes,
I know the meaning of
"Obianuju"
but your daughter's name
is not that of a European saint
and the priest needs to be able
to baptize her without
bringing in darkness.

Your names
are heathen
and Jesus
needs holy names.

We are tired of carrying our fathers' sins.
We are sick of cleaning the wounds of our mothers.
Here, we are growing new flesh in pain.
Here, we are sinking our teeth into earth,
coming up with new histories.

You are a collection of civil wars
born with your mother
cursing you to set her free
your father never returned
after your mother's first trimester.

You are a land filled with
half-empty bottles of promises
and half-vagabond blood.

You are a quiet distress
a disappearing act
when souls utter
"love"

You are a fragile piece of work
a monument of regrets
a bastard soul

A hurting country.

You asked your father
how you should say your name.
He said if they cannot say your name
then they must try,
but you will not soften it,
you will not break the magic apart,
you will not be ashamed of it.

Ijeoma Umebinyuo

Iya Femi

Listen to me
I was alive long before the civil war
before this was even Nigeria
I am a Yoruba woman
my ancestors were Yoruba
forget this foolish label the white man has given us
let us leave that matter for another day
you are asking why I am walking around like this?
my daughter, do you know how many children
have passed through this womb?
I bless my Orishas for keeping me
I have earned the right to walk around
showing the village my gray hair
and my flat breasts
my children and old age milked dry
my husband is long gone
too many years with that man
I was his third wife, his jewel
he just couldn't get enough of my young blood
I travelled to the Osun river to offer sacrifices
there, my waist beads would be blessed
my husband never married after me
bless his heart
pass me that alligator pepper
what did you ask me again?
I don't know where Femi is
do I look like I keep my son tied to my waist?

Yellow Fever

I am woman enough to know
you do not force
womanhood out of girls

That you do not shame
the bodies of girls,
forcing them
to carry themselves like an apology,
to hold sorry on their lips

So, on the day Uchenna
is offered bleaching cream
she will know her skin like moonless nights
is a beautiful color to carry with pride.

Sins of the fathers

you desecrated the shrines of our fathers
you pushed our tongue, stole our culture
paraded your wickedness as my savior
you refused the right to let me own my narrative
you butchered our names
you brought war on our land
you call my people "savages"
you stole our histories
and wear them proudly in your museums
you wash away our achievements
you carry it as yours
you "discover" what was already mine
you plant puppets, assassinating our leaders
you desecrated the shrines of my mothers
when we worshipped nature, you laughed at us
now, you want to carry our ways, learn from us
we refuse to write softness into our stories
for you to feel comfortable
we refuse to let anyone but us own our narrative
we refuse to believe your lies again
you will not spit in the face of our fathers
and think his children will sit quietly.

Anger

Please be still,
I am writing you
into a poem.

Just a minute,
let me remove
the thunder
inside your veins
.

Ijeoma Umebinyuo

my demons
turned to angels
after i understood
that the pain
only polished me
for a better reflection.

Your lover sped away,
leaving tire marks on your skin.
You have resolved to eating
yesterday for breakfast.

I watch you gather your memories
like firewood,
warming yourself
for yet another lonely night.

Ijeoma Umebinyuo

Trigger

He said
"How can you be a virgin?
There are no virgins in Nigeria!"
As he laughed his laugh
you watch him quietly
He puts his fingers in
as you flinch
"Be a big girl," you told yourself
At twenty-five, you should know
a man will leave
if you do not offer him some sugah

So, he unzips
and you hear yourself cry
But you never made a sound
he will not understand

He said
"How can you be a virgin?
There are no virgins in Nigeria!"
And you hold on
rushing to the bathroom
to scrub his smell away

Now, you plant cactus on your skin
preparing for the men
who will come
for some of your sugah.

Scarred

The boy from Swaziland
looks at you with lust.
He has taught you how to
use your tongue
to taste his skin.

When he kisses you
he finds the ocean
in your heat
as you shift the sky,
calling his name.

The boy from Swaziland
has taught you how to love boys
with skinny fingers
and caramel skin
that burns with memories.

You spill his name on his blanket,
you watch him smile,
he sleeps, you trace his scar,
he flinches
and begins to cry.

Even in his sleep,
a man never forgets
how his mother died.

Splinter

Your father does not
carry pain like most do.

He puts it in bottles
and throws it at your mother
till she screams for God,
kneeling in church
seeking refuge in the arms
of the unknown.

Your father
came back from the war;

now he's always crying at night

and without saying a word

your mother strips naked
as he
holds her body,
whispering

"thank you"
before drifting off to sleep.

Pardon me
for breaking
myself
in half
for you.

Things we lost in the fire

The gentle reminders
as you leave some patches of your spirit
around the corners of my soul,
freeing yet binding me to you.
The way my name rolled off your tongue
as though you were whispering it to God.

Late-night calls
as you peel words,
sprinkling them with desire
for me to taste.

Forgive me, how did your soul forget so soon?
The way we held on to heaven,
carrying our moans as offerings to The Universe
scratching our souls, mapping our conquest.

The way we thought
our world would never end.

Invisible

She scanned through the magazine
for girls who looked like her
with deeper hues,
flat nose, and thick hair.

The day she turned fifteen
she scrubbed herself with bleach
while screaming for God,
whispering over and over again
"the darker the skin,
the deeper the struggle"
releasing a sigh
that made her soul shake.

Ijeoma Umebinyuo

You must let the pain visit.
You must allow it teach you.
You must not allow it overstay.

Weight of sadness

You apologize for
how you carry your
mother's loneliness
quietly
between your teeth.

You apologize for
how you carry your
father's sins
inside your blood.

You forgot
how to carry yourself
away from the histories
that threaten to break you open,
leaving you with grief
and unbearable weight of emptiness.

Tell me, apart from the sadness
thick as smog
living inside your chest
tell me the last time
you held your face
and saw love
staring back at you.

Ijeoma Umebinyuo

How does destroying yourself
prove your worth to others?

She was always a wildflower—
even her sadness, like water,
helped her grow.

quench

my body still tastes of him
as my mouth
says his name at night
the heaviness in my chest
still lingers
my thighs still seek him
i am clinging to memories
even in water,
i am parched.

Ginikachukwu

kinky hair
tough hair
rich melanin
auntie is writing
about how i danced
when you were born

auntie is writing
about how you made
the house so warm
with your infectious laughter
kinky hair
tough hair
rich melanin

auntie knows
auntie knows
the world might show you
as unwanted
auntie knows
you are pure gold
infectious laughter
loud neon smile
rich melanin
auntie knows
it might get tough sometimes

Ijeoma Umebinyuo

Ginikachukwu, find me, find me
and if i am no longer on earth,
please know this:
auntie has written enough poems
to speak of your beauty
forever.

Children of the wars

Please,
give him something
for his nightmares

The child keeps
calling me father.

Ijeoma Umebinyuo

freedom looks better on you

may we be able to tell the difference
between peacekeepers
and
mercenaries.

if war comes knocking
and the sea buries more bodies than land,
may we know the names of the dead.

each name a prayer before God.

kneel in the middle of your room in Los Angeles
cry for the dead bodies that look like you
tell me, how many missing girls
found with bombs strapped to their dead bodies
will make the blood of your country boil?
may we be able to tell the difference
between peacekeepers
and
mercenaries.

Summer of lies and blood

It seems the cracks
in the pavements
down in America
are revealing the bodies
of young black souls

Ijeoma Umebinyuo

make no mistake:
these revolutionaries
will turn prayers
and kisses
into gunpowder-filled ink
for the liberation

lover,
wrap my poems
around your tongue.

Ijeoma Umebinyuo

darling, just because you ignore a star
does not mean it stops shining. even on you.

Morning Liturgy

There is so much beauty within
beauty attached to my names
beauty attached to my skin
beauty attached to the grace in my walk
beauty attached to my tongue
beauty attached to my flaws
Look at me, brewing stars in my skin.

Ijeoma Umebinyuo

I told the priest
"My God is a black woman."
He poured holy water on me
and scheduled me for an exorcism.

The morning in your voice
gently wakes my soul
You gather my pain
throwing it back to yesterday
Kiss me again
let me pick the sonnets
from your lips

Ijeoma Umebinyuo

I want to write about
women who clap their hands
women who sing loud
women who gossip
sitting in their stores,
avoiding the scorching heat
I want to write about women
who love colors with patterns
who sit on the motorcycle
with their legs to the side,
women who live quiet loud lives
who hawk in the streets
with sweets and food
to feed their children
and speak in broken English,
like the woman who sells soap
or the woman who sews beautiful dresses
I want to write about
women who scream with joy
at the sight of you
dancing for joy
at your arrival
I want to write about
women who pray for me
in a language so beautiful
english will bow.

Twenty-six

Three days after you turned twenty-six, you pick up the phone to hear her speak. Your voice is laced with tiredness, the kind that grows weary of men who only come to take. The kind of tiredness you spend three days on the bed wishing away. The kind that kneels on the floor, screaming for help without voicing a word.

Three days after you turned twenty-six, your Igbo mother, with her voice squeezing into the telephone, tells you about your birth. You listen to her call you her miracle child. You try not to break down.

Somehow, she knows. She says softly, "My daughter, it will hurt, it will hurt but you will be okay. E nu go?" Gently, you suck your pride and begin to shake as you cry. You know for the first time in your life, you know even your mother has been here before.

You know her voice has been stretched. You know that before your father, there was a man who broke her so badly her sisters gathered, sucking their teeth, healing her with words, feeding her spoonfuls of love.

You slowly bathe yourself. Today, you will apply your red lipstick without calling out his name. Today, you will not feed your pillow more tears.

Today, you will win.

Chetachi

Chetachi, for night him go come tell mi sai mak i no
talk, him sai if i sai anything na village i go go! Oga go
come almst evry night when all deir pikin don slep, him
go leve auntie for bed to mak mi cri.

Anytme when him dey on top. Cheta, i go rember
when me and you dey village, when we dey laugh with
Okwudiri and all of dem before whn oga start i dey cri,
i dey beg now i no say anythn now i no cri i swear to
God.

Cheta since i comes here my mind never smiles madam
no let me go school she go flog me if i no speak good
enlish i wan speaks like her children na children auntie
dey call dem but e dey hard.

For nights when oga no come disturb me i go read
their novels for boys quarters way i dey stay i wan read,
i dey see how their schildren dey read i wan read and
speaks like them i dey try, but, Cheta, e hard.

For sunday i go floow dem go church. madam no like
to miss church, she dey get holy ghost for church, she
go dey speaks in tnuges!

As madm dey speak oga dey altar dey read bible.

You are crying
and the angels sit,
comforting God
telling her to stop
feeling so pained.
"Where does it hurt?"
they ask.
She points to you.

Ijeoma Umebinyuo

You are your mother's amen
to all her prayers
the calm to her trembling soul.
She gathers your happiness,
rubbing it on her skin
till she begins to glow.

Hurting

tell me about the pain
what triggers the nightmares
how many times have you
cut sleep to stare at your mirror
screaming at your reflection?

tell me about the days
when your body refuses to move
as you carry your sighs
spreading it across your bed
muttering prayers to yourself
begging for your salvation.

tell me about the night
you held the phone close
screaming for help
without making a sound
wiping away all your smiles
revealing the true color of your soul.

tell me about your scars
tell me about your pain
from collarbone to thighs
from knotted nerves
to decaying hope
tell me about it all.

Ijeoma Umebinyuo

When your body remembers,
how do you carry her back into love?

Offerings

There you were at thirteen, tracing back your age
to find truths you tried burying
tracing two years back
the smell of the dark room
tracing three years back
the sound of your siblings playing outside
tracing four years back
he said, "Do not tell anyone.
No one will believe you"
tracing four years back
your mother asking why you hurt so much.

You quietly swallow the truth:
he offered you darkness
at twenty-two he touched you
you flinched
at twenty-four he asked,
"So, how come you've never
had sex or even a boyfriend?"

Your response
should have been
because a child given darkness as a gift
cannot comprehend how to let the sun in
without thinking
it would take from her again.
I am writing for
the women
who keep kneeling
screaming at their phone

you shame the bodies of your daughters,
forcing them into hating themselves
imperfect daughters
who make their mothers
kneel and ask God
to make
them normal
visit home without showing
their scars.
your daughter
hides it well,
all the sadness
all the grief
she carries
inside her blood
with her smile
with her hello
with her religion.
your daughter sat
across from me
spreading a lifetime
of "a disappointment
of a daughter"
and i watched her break apart,
unveiling her pain.
so forgive her
for loving men
whose delight
come from
forcing sadness inside her

so forgive her
for never loving herself
enough.
and
your daughter sat
across from me.
showing me a frightened girl
who keeps disappointing her mother.

Ijeoma Umebinyuo

Chewing Flowers

I am writing for the women who were once
girls judging themselves through the eyes of
souls who couldn't comprehend their light

I am writing for the women who stammered just to
speak and who forced themselves into silence when
ugly words were once thrown at them

I am writing for the women who keep kneeling
screaming at their phone as lovers leave

as friends depart

I am writing for all these women who still show up
with a smile

after battling their demons the night before

I am also writing for the women who do not smile the
next day. women who need a day or two to
recover from the brutalities of the world

woman, sin.
sinner, woman.
man, judge.
woman, sin.
man, judge.
sinner, woman.
Silence, woman.

Ijeoma Umebinyuo

Poem No. 6

I will teach my daughter
how to be a lioness at night
and a dove in the morning

how to be so gentle with herself
and sing herself back into love
with poems, with dance, with tea,
with silence and solitude

Children of a Lesser God

He sometimes forgets
But then he remembers
The smell, the unlit room
The ways his body carried secrets
Memories that burn it
Setting fire to the holy parts of God
He became familiar with pain.

She sometimes forgets
But then, she remembers
The way she held guilt between her teeth
And inside her body, drying her bones
As though she pulled herself away
From all the yellow.

We sometimes forget
Then we remember
We weep and hold ourselves
Like a sacrifice to the darkness.

Someday, we will learn how
To stop hurting ourselves
Because pain is not
The only emotion
Worthy of our being.

The Last Poem

I came to you
as a wildflower,
as a woman who passed
through different stages
of her womanhood
to know not even the
sweetest man
deserves my silence.

You are not holy water.

Flawed as I am,
I was not a sin.

The depth of void

You must not eat anger,
carry their sins,
or cover yourself with hate.

You must not scream or
drag your heart across your room
till your voice is hoarse from pain.

You must not inflict more pain
into the wounds or pray away the demon
they have forced you to believe
lives inside you.

You must not howl at the moon
nor curse the daylight or your reflection.

You must not try to forget
when your past still bleeds
you must not try to be strong
you must remember
never to do all these
when the memories visit.

You must remember
to feel every emotion
but this guilt;
you must wash it away
with everything you have got.

Ijeoma Umebinyuo

At home,
older women
trace my roots
by staring at my face.

Sometimes, they see my father,
sometimes they see my mother
and sometimes, they see their friend
My grandmother.

Home

You remember the name of your grandfathers and your grandmothers and the names of your uncles. You tell them the names of your aunties, like the one who wiped your butt as a child and sang you to sleep. You remember them. You remember your mother, her eyes and how she looked at you when she wanted the truth. You remember how she looked at you when you were thirteen and she bought your first bra, how she was smiling at you. You remember the day she told you how to count the days, to know you have become a woman when the blood first came. You remember it all. You remember how she couldn't finish college but woke you up every morning to prepare you for school. You remember your father. You remember how he always called you with love, how he tells everyone his daughter will be great, you remember how the job hurt his knees but he never complained. You remember your grandfather and the stories he always told you. You remember their names, you remember your village. So, when the darkness visits, when home seems so far away, start calling all their names and I promise they will come to keep you company. Remember whose daughter you are; speak with pride like you have been taught. Do not lower your head, just like your father taught you. Do not stutter, do not break apart. There are so many ancestors back home praying for you. Do not let the distance break your heart.

Ijeoma Umebinyuo

Ada

Last night,
I asked my grandmother
what to do with all the pain.
"Wash it clean with love,"
she said.

tonight
there is rain
there is poetry
there is music
and here
trying to rise again
is your beautiful life.

Ka chi fo

And love said:
come, let me teach you
how to smile again.

Questions for Ada

CPSIA information can be obtained
at www.ICGtesting.com
Printed in the USA
LVHW020843200622
721643LV00002B/227

9 781505 984347